T0381197

AuthorHouse™
1663 Liberty Drive
Bloomington, IN 47403
www.authorhouse.com
Phone: 1 (800) 839-8640

© 2015 Maureen Baggett. All rights reserved.

No part of this book may be reproduced, stored in a retrieval system,
or transmitted by any means without the written permission of the author.

Published by AuthorHouse 3/27/2015

ISBN: 978-1-5049-0134-5 (sc)
978-1-5049-0135-2 (e)

Print information available on the last page.

Any people depicted in stock imagery provided by Thinkstock are models,
and such images are being used for illustrative purposes only.
Certain stock imagery © Thinkstock.

This book is printed on acid-free paper.

Because of the dynamic nature of the Internet, any web addresses or links contained in this book may have changed
since publication and may no longer be valid. The views expressed in this work are solely those of the author and do not
necessarily reflect the views of the publisher, and the publisher hereby disclaims any responsibility for them.

Nana's Wish

by Maureen Baggett

Edited by: Stella Gregor

Maureen (Nana) 1955
Age 8

Odessa 2014
Age 8

Nana's Wish

Odessa woke up slowly, yawning and stretching her arms as she always did in the morning. Carrot, her stuffed animal, was just where he always was, cozily near her head, but something warm was very snug against both of her sides. Cautiously, she opened her eyes and looked straight into the brown eyes of a girl just her size.

"Hi!" the other girl said. "I was wishing you would be here soon."

"Hello. Your eyes are just like my Nana's."

"Of course, silly. It's because I am your Nana, but I'm eight years old now, too. You're in bed with your Aunt Martha and me in Maryland in 1955. You get to spend all day with us. I kept wishing and wishing and wishing and finally my wish came true! I'm so excited. Now, get up, sleepy head. It's a new day! There is only one bathroom and if we don't hurry Sam and Eliott will hog it. Hurry! Hurry!"

The girls rushed out of bed and were into the bathroom in a jiffy. Soon with teeth and hair brushed they came back to the small pink bedroom and started to dress for the day. Martha was very happy to see Odessa.

"Maureen told me she was wishing for you to visit, but I told her not to get her hopes up. Oh no, Odessa," she quickly added when she saw Odessa slipping on some pants and a tee-shirt. "You're going to school with us. You have to wear a dress."

"But my legs might get cold in school, if I wear a dress and what if I want to go on the jungle gym?" asked Odessa.

"Odessa, it's school. You have to wear a dress!" Nana insisted. "It doesn't matter if you are cold or hot. You're a girl. All girls wear dresses to school." She thought for a second. "You mean where you come from, you don't wear dresses to school? How strange! I can't even imagine it! Anyway, don't worry about being cold. It's May and very hot. We'll jump rope at recess. The Gym is at the high school and there isn't any jungle in Maryland."

"Okay." Odessa put on a skirt and top that were in a bag that mysteriously had come on the trip with her and the three girls tromped down the stairs to answer the call to breakfast.

Including Odessa there were seven people around the table. Of course, they welcomed Odessa, because she was a part of their family no matter what year she would come into it. That is the way of wishes. Nana's mother, who would later become Odessa's Grammy, was at one end of the table. Nana's father was at the other end. Her brothers, Sam and Eliott sat on one side of the table. Martha sat closest to her father on the other side, and Nana sat near her mother. There was a platter with a pile of fried eggs, a platter of bacon and a steady supply of toast. Though Odessa liked bacon, she wasn't sure she could eat the gooey eggs, even though the others were digging in. She noticed that each girl took one egg, one piece of bacon and two pieces of toast. Everyone had a glass of milk in front of them. Odessa thought she saw something floating in her milk. It was a piece of grass! Ugh. No way was she going to drink that.

"Oh sorry, Odessa," Nana said as she fished out the grass. "Sometimes when the milk is strained, something falls back in. I'll trade with you." She switched glasses and began to drink the milk as though there had never been any grass in it.

"You mean this milk came from one of your cows?"

"Oh yeah," Sam, ten years old, replied. "I milked Betsy last night."

"Don't say, 'yeah' Sam," his mother admonished him.

"Mommy, all the kids do!"

"And don't say 'kid'! A 'kid' is a baby goat!"

"Mommy, I ain't gonna say anything if you keep telling me what not to say," he teased.

"Sam! What am I going to do with you? Don't say ain't! Now go brush your teeth or you'll be late for school. Martha, go get the hairbrush so I can braid your hair. Odessa and Maureen, go wash your hands. Eliott, aren't you glad you're just barely 5 and you get to stay home with your Mommy?"

"Yeah," Sam told him. "Martha and I went to kindergarten in D.C., but now that we live on the farm, you and Maureen get to stay with Mommy for years and years and years until First Grade, you lucky dog!"

While Martha's hair was being tightly braided, Nana and Odessa prepared four brown paper lunch bags. In each one they put an apple, two homemade chocolate chip cookies, and a tongue and mustard sandwich wrapped loosely in waxed paper. Odessa was again wondering about how hungry she would be by the end of this day. She looked longingly at the other cookies on the counter. Nana wrote each person's first name in pencil on a paper bag.

Martha 12   Sam 10   Eliott 5

Sam only carried his lunch, but Martha and Nana carried brief cases with their school things. Nana seemed proud that hers was red plaid. The three girls started down the long farm lane first. Sam was playing with four dogs in the front yard. There were no houses anywhere to be seen so Odessa knew that the dogs belonged to Nana's family. She couldn't wait to play with them when she got home from school. On one side of the lane tobacco was planted and on the other side was corn. Martha explained to Odessa that earlier in the spring Martha and Nana's mother had sat on a tobacco planter pulled by a tractor. Each of them had a stack of plants in their laps. The tobacco planter would dig a trough in the ground. Martha would place a plant in the hole. Then Nana's mother would place one. After each plant went in the ground the planter sent water after it, and the dirt would fall back into place over the roots. The boys would follow behind and stamp their feet around the little plant to make sure it was securely in the ground. Nana, who had trouble staying out too long in the hot Maryland sun, got to stay at the house and do dishes, make beds, and fold clothes which was lots easier than the hot dirty work outside. She often got teased about it.

As the three girls ambled down the lane, all of the sudden they saw the big yellow school bus. OH NO!!! Where was Sam?

"Buuuussssssss!!!!" Martha yelled loudly. Nana looked embarrassed. She and Odessa ran the last yards to the bus as it stopped for the girls.

"Don't worry!" said the bus driver to Odessa. "This isn't the first time. Luckily, this is the last stop. I just turn around and pick him up on the way back. He's a rascal, that one."

Sure enough after the bus turned around the driver opened the door and an out of breath Sam grinned at the driver and crossed the road to swing onto the bus. "That was a close one," said the driver with a smile.

On the way to the school Odessa noticed a bunch of barefoot African American children walking to a small old building close to the road. "Is that your school?" She asked.

A child behind her snickered when he heard her question. Nana leaned close to her and whispered. "No, Odessa. That's where the colored children go to school, but last year there was a big court case that all the grownups are talking about. Soon we will all go to school together. Right now they go to that school, and there isn't even a bathroom or a sink! Pretty awful, huh? It's best not to talk about it at school though, 'cause some of the other children don't even realize it's wrong. It can get people all upset. We only talk about it at home."

Odessa sat back in her seat to think. 1955 sure was a strange time to live. The African American kids were called 'colored' and went to a different school. Everyone talked a different way, couldn't wear comfortable clothes to school, and couldn't even say the things they wanted to say. She was feeling pretty happy that she lived 60 years in the future, and she wasn't even including the food situation!

The yellow school bus pulled into the school with 15 other buses. The children got off all at once and walked immediately into school. Teenagers stayed on the buses and went on to their school which was farther away. Odessa tried to figure out how everyone knew where to go and why no one got lost. Nana showed her a long narrow hall in the back of the classroom that was called a cloak closet. They left their lunches there and then went to Nana's desk. There were 35 desks in the class lined up in five rows of seven facing the teacher. Odessa was to sit in a vacant desk next to Nana. No sooner was everyone seated than a bell rang.

c)noonie/Dreamstime.com. Classroom Photo

The teacher, Miss Gardner, who had been standing silently in the front of the classroom put her hand over her heart, faced the flag and began to say the pledge to the flag. Odessa scrambled to catch up as she realized that all 35 children did the same. As she focused on the flag, she noticed that it looked odd. She counted. There were only 48 stars! Where were the other two? Odessa reminded herself to ask Nana about it later.

c)Stillfix/Dreamstime.com -Flag and Blackboard photo

Immediately afterwards the teacher folded her hands, bowed her head and with the class said the Lord's Prayer.

As the teacher finally began to speak to the class, Odessa took a moment to look around. Miss Gardner wore a long silky dark dress, cinched in at her waist with a slender black belt. Shiny stockings led down to sensible dark high heeled shoes. When she wasn't speaking her mouth was pinched shut and her eyes managed the children by simply a glance here and there. The alphabet was placed around the room over the blackboard. On the two bulletin boards were a job chart and a calendar.

As Martha had told her, all of the girls wore dresses, but oddly all of the boys wore long pants. Not one boy was wearing shorts! No one looked cool on this hot Maryland day despite the windows being open all along one wall of the classroom.

Soon, eight people got up from their desks and went to the front of the room and sat on chairs around the teacher.

"What are they doing?" whispered Odessa.

"Shhh…You'll get me in trouble and we'll have to stand in the corner. It's reading group. We're s'pposed to do our spelling. Look at the blackboard."

Odessa looked up at the board and saw the schedule of the day printed neatly.

9:15 -9:45 Red Group
9:45-10:15 Blue Group
10:15-10:35 Recess
10:35 -11:10 Green Group
11:15-12:00 Arithmetic Lesson
12:00- 12:30 Lunch
12:30- 1:00 Recess
1:00- 1:30 Social Studies
1:30-2:00 Penmanship
2:00-2:15 Spelling Bee
2:30-2:45 Recess
2:45-3:00 Story
During Reading groups you are to do your Spelling and Arithmetic.

Spelling P. 145-148
Arithmetic P. 232-235 All work must be neatly done or you will stay in from recess.

Odessa noticed that the other students had reached inside their desks. She looked in hers where she found a paperback book titled Second Grade Speller. The first page was about changing words by adding a silent e. The words were: tub, can, pin, rob, cub, kit, tap, and man. Easy, Peasy. Odessa quickly made the new list. Tube, cane, pine, robe, cube, kite, tape, mane. Wow! Back home, her spelling list included the word 'pathological'. Nana sure had it easy.

The next instruction said that words ending in y after a consonant changed to -ies when he, she, and it were talking. The words were: fry, cry, try, worry, carry, hurry copy, and dry. Odessa had no trouble writing the new words: fries, cries, tries, worries, carries, hurries, copies, and dries. She looked over at Nana. Nana winked. The next task was to put all those words in alphabetical order. Piece of cake. They called this school! But before she knew it, Nana took her by the hand and led her up to the front of the room. Evidently, she was in the Blue reading Group. This could be interesting.

There were ten children in the group. They sat in a circle. Miss Gardner started by asking them if they had ever thought about giants and ogres and whether they could be real. Unfortunately, though, you had to raise your hand before you could talk, and before they got to her turn, Odessa forgot what she wanted to say! She noticed that Nana didn't raise her hand, but just listened to everything and stared down at the book as though she wanted to eat it. Odessa understood, because she was pretty hungry, herself. One girl in the group, Joanne, seemed to want to talk, non-stop and Miss Gardner had to tell her to think about other people. Joanne turned red, but it wasn't a blush. It was anger! Interesting! Finally, they were allowed to open to page 302, but they were told not to read ahead. Each person read several paragraphs and then another person read a few. Of course the story was about a giant and an ogre. Big surprise! Every now and then Miss Gardner would ask questions about what was happening as though no one had read anything. Some people read very slowly and stumbled over the words. They needed lots of help from Miss Gardner. Odessa noticed that Nana was keeping track of where the group was reading, but was secretly reading way ahead. She was tricky, because she managed to stay on the same page, but only just. Nana, never volunteered to answer a question, but was always ready when she was asked. Strangely, Nana never answered in her real voice, but in a quiet little mouse voice. Odder and odder! Odessa had even more questions than Miss Gardner! Finally, the bell rang, the whole class leapt up, and the excruciating reading group ended.

Miss Gardner's voice also erupted. "Your teacher dismisses not the bell! " Everyone sat down tensely on the edge of their seats until she called out, "dismissed!"

"Whew!" Nana said to Odessa. "That was the longest morning of my life! I kept waiting and waiting for recess. These are my best friends, Lindy, Patty, and Sandy. Oh and this is Joanne. Girls, Odessa is just visiting our school for today."

Joanne had run up behind the others. "Do you want to jump rope? I can show Odessa all the tricks. I'm the best at everything. Aren't I"

"You are really good. That is for sure," answered Patty. "But we want to show Odessa the whole playground just like we show everyone who is new."

"What's to show? See-saw, swings, merry-go-round, trees to climb, baseball diamond and done. Now, let's jump rope"

"Oh come on, Joanne. Don't be such a Sad Sack," complained Lindy. "We'll jump rope at the next recess."

"Actually," Odessa said. "I want to know more about Nana. Do you have any stories about her?"

"Actually," mocked Joanne. "I want to know why you call Maureen, Nana. HER NAME IS MAUREEN."

"Hey, stop being mean, Joanne," Lindy and Nana said at the same time and then laughed together. Nana continued, "She has called me Nana all her life. For some reason when she first saw me, she started calling me Nana, and she hasn't stopped. I've gotten used to it. But just for the record, the rest of you can keep calling me, Maureen."

They continued on toward the swings holding hands, but Joanne still wanted all eyes on her. "I've got a story about her. She didn't say one word for the first six weeks of first grade. We all thought she was a big dummy or something!"

"We did not!" defended Sandy. "We didn't even notice that she wasn't saying anything, but I guess the teacher, nice Miss Fowler called her mom about it."

"Let me tell this part," called out Lindy from the line of linked hands. "I'm the star of this part. Maureen is just really, really, really shy. I thought I was shy, but then along came Maureen. Anyway, Miss Fowler called Mrs. Robertson, Maureen's mom. Then one day we heard someone's high heels coming down the hallway outside our classroom. Clomp. Clomp. Clomp. Those shoes were really loud. We all thought someone really important like the principal was coming. Then a face looked in through the little window of the door and Miss Fowler went into the hall for a few minutes. The face was Mrs. Robertson! When Miss Fowler came back in she moved my seat next to Maureen's seat."

"Yes," exclaimed Nana happily. "Then Lindy started talking to me nicely and I couldn't be rude and not answer her. My days of not talking were over, but I still have the shyness problem."

"Well, you should just work on that." Joanne butted in. "Anyway she didn't really call Maureen's mother, because Maureen's family doesn't even have a telephone. They had to call her grandmother, who had to run across a field and get her. Then Maureen's mother had to borrow a car to come to school, because they don't have a car either. Well, the daddy must have one, but he was at work. Last one on the swings is a rotten egg! I'm going to swing all the way over the top, today. Who wants to push me first?"

The other girls pretended they hadn't heard everything that Joanne had said. "She sure is mean," Odessa said to Nana, but Nana didn't seem to hear.

The girls took turns swinging and climbing trees for the rest of the recess, but it was over way too soon. When the bell rang they ran to stand in line and filed in to wait at the bathroom and drinking fountain. The water tasted warm and bitter. Odessa used it just to rinse out her mouth. She wasn't sure if it was good for her to drink, even though the rest of the children seemed to not mind at all.

Back in the classroom Odessa looked at the schedule and realized it was time to tackle Arithmetic. Oh no! Back at home she was working on the fives tables and it was not easy. She turned to the assigned page in the book. What? It was practicing carrying numbers while adding. What could be easier? Wait a minute. Wait a minute. There were….50 problems! What was the point in having 50 problems? She looked over at Nana. Zip. Zip. Zip. Her pencil was moving like lightning. Odessa started moving her pencil just as fast. Just as her hand was cramped and eraser dust was everywhere, the green group came back to their seats. Odessa looked at the clock. It was time for the Arithmetic Lesson and she was only halfway through the problems. What was going to happen? Miss Gardner always looked very stern and she looked even more so as she stood in front of the class with her hands folded.

"Now it is time for the arithmetic lesson. Today we are going to talk again about carrying numbers over when you are adding two columns. You have had some time to practice at your desks and you will have time to finish later this afternoon or tomorrow morning."

What a lucky break for the class! There was a big sigh from more than one person whose hand had been covering an incomplete page. Miss Gardner then showed the class how to do two problems on the board and asked for volunteers to come to the board and show the problems they had done. How boring! This went on for several minutes until Odessa noticed that not only was Nana not volunteering, she was slithering down in her chair to be as unnoticeable as possible. Did she really think Miss Gardner would forget she was there? Evidently it worked. She was not called on! Nana was staring at a boy fiddling in his desk across the room. He seemed to be rolling something back and forth inside of his desk. Oops! It fell out of his desk and rolled across the floor right up to Miss Gardner's foot! She sure noticed that!

"Frankie Miller! What is this?"

"It looks like a baseball, Miss Gardner."

"It is a baseball with your brother's name in big letters on it!"

"Yes, Miss Gardner."

"Frankie Miller, you know that this is not the first time that you have been in trouble in this classroom."

"Yes."

"Yes, what"

"Yes, Ma'am"

"You've been in the corner many times. I've called your mother. We've talked in the hall. I've rapped your knuckles. You have not mended your ways. You know what I told you would happen if things didn't change."

"Yes, Ma'am."

"March right down to the Principal, young man!"

Frankie slowly slipped out of his chair and walked to the door dragging his feet at each step as though he hoped that Miss Gardner would take mercy on him once more. The whole class seemed to shudder with each move he made. When he cleared the doorway they could hear him sobbing as he walked down the hall. It was hard to pretend to go back to walking normally up to the board to do arithmetic problems. Everyone was very relieved to hear the lunch bell ring.

"Nana, Nana," Odessa said quickly. "What is going to happen to poor Frankie Miller? He was crying. I felt so awful for him."

"I think the Principal will spank him. That's what they say happens when you go to the Principal. Mommy says that the Principal isn't allowed to spank us, but that the other children are allowed to be spanked at school. Daddy called the school and told them they weren't allowed to spank us. I don't know how that works, but anyway once Sam got in trouble and he got spanked at home when the Principal called."

"What did Sam do wrong?"

"I wish I could remember. Anyway, Frankie just has a terrible time paying attention. He is always doing interesting things in his desk or drawing really great pictures. He never looks at the teacher. He can't read and he can't do arithmetic at all. He also misses lots of school. It's pretty boring when he isn't here. Let's get our lunches from the cloakroom."

"Why do they call it the cloakroom? I don't see any cloaks."

"That's funny. I don't even know what a cloak is! People must have just always called it that. The old part of the school is very, very old, and the names for things just stayed the same, I guess. I'm really hungry. Are you?"

Odessa thought of the tongue sandwich with mustard which didn't seem as nasty as it had this morning, but the cookies were what she was really looking forward to. They went to a big room called the auditorium with a stage at one end. Big tables had been set up and the girls found room to sit near Patty, Lindy, and Sandy. Soon, Joanne came over and squeezed everyone over to make room for her.

"Hello, everybody! I bet Frankie gets switched 500 times!" Joanne said with relish. "He deserves it, too. He should have been paying attention. What a retard!"

"Joanne," Sandy started, but she couldn't continue. Everyone knew that Sandy had a sister who was often called 'retarded' by mean children like Joanne, but not everyone realized how much it hurt.

"My mommy says, 'if you can't say something nice, don't say anything at all'," Nana broke in hesitantly, "I kind of think that's a good policy. Frankie has a sore enough bottom without us saying mean things about him, too."

"Well, I know you'd rather talk about Richard Tabler, wouldn't you?" Joanne answered. "You love him so, so much!"

Nana blushed. "Well, I am going to marry him when I grow up," she announced under her breath as they gathered their trash.

"I don't think so." Odessa whispered following the other girls out to the playground.

"Okay, this time we jump rope. Who is going to turn the rope? I'll jump first, because I want Odessa to see how great a jumper I am." Joanne announced, because she didn't mind taking charge and getting right to what she wanted to do.

Lindy and Odessa took the ends of the rope and started turning the rope. Odessa noticed that on another part of the playground Martha and some other sixth grade girls were jumping Double Dutch. It looked very hard. Sam was playing kickball with other fourth grade boys.

Joanne jumped in and the girls started chanting:

"Teddy Bear, Teddy Bear
Touch the ground!
Teddy Bear, Teddy Bear
Turn around!"

As Joanne jumped she touched the ground, turned around, reached up high, and waved good-bye. She was really very good at it. When Joanne jumped out, Nana jumped in and Joanne changed places with Lindy. It turned out all the girls were good at jumping and doing the tricks that went with it. After the girls each had a chance to do Teddy Bear, they did other chants while jumping. Everyone was out of breath when recess was over.

Odessa was hot and sweaty. The water still tasted just as bad as it had earlier, but it was much more welcome!

As the children came back into the classroom Odessa looked at the clock. It was 1 o'clock, time for Social Studies. Miss Gardner came to the front of the room and started talking about a man named Doctor Mudd who lived long ago on a farm nearby. As the story went, he had lived during the War Between the States and had been a southern sympathizer. When John Wilkes Booth assassinated President Lincoln, Booth broke his leg in his escape. Despite the broken leg, Booth and his co-conspirator, John Herold rode on horseback all the way from Washington D.C to Dr. Mudd's house to have the leg set. The ride must have taken many hours. When they arrived at his house at four in the morning, Dr. Mudd set John Wilkes Booth's leg, let him shave his moustache off, and told him of another place to go that would welcome him.

Odessa smiled to herself. She had read a book about the Civil War and knew that Miss Gardner was calling it the 'War Between the States', because she still felt like she was living in a southern state even though almost a hundred years had passed! When Odessa looked around the classroom, though, she was amazed that the other children were spellbound by the story and taking it in as absolute truth. She wondered whether Dr. Mudd would be hero or villain.

Miss Gardner continued to tell that Dr. Mudd had been arrested several days later and sentenced to life imprisonment. He claimed that he had never met John Wilkes Booth before that day and had set the broken bone, because it was his obligation as a doctor. Only one jury vote saved him from being sentenced to death as other conspirators were. On the way to jail, however, he confessed to his guard that he had indeed been guilty. At the jail the prison doctor died in a yellow fever outbreak, and Dr. Mudd took over his duties and saved many lives. Four years later he was pardoned by President Andrew Johnson.

During the whole time Miss Gardner spoke, she didn't ask the children for their opinions or ask if they had any questions. It was very different from a lesson that Odessa would have in 2014! Odessa had lots to think about. She wondered if the children thought that Dr. Mudd was a hero, because there was an historic sign nearby pointing to his house. Was he a villain because he was in on an assassination? Was he a hero because he was a doctor and helped so many people? Does a war change what a hero is and what a villain is?

But there was no more time to think. Funny lined paper was being handed out by Miss Gardner. It was the penmanship lesson. The first half of the fifteen minutes was spent practicing going up and down with the pencil. For the next fifteen minutes they were to do the 0's to get ready for learning to write in cursive. The goal was to keep between the lines, and it was harder than it looked. Miss Gardner passed up and down the rows with a ruler in her hands looking very stern. At one point she made Joanne go stand with her nose to the corner, because she had been whispering "Fatty, fatty, two by four can't get through the bathroom door" to a heavy little boy sitting next to her.

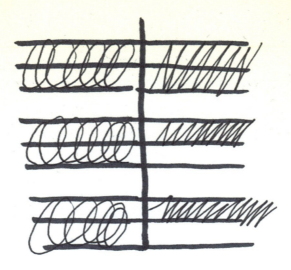

Just then a loud siren rang through the building. It was much louder than the bell that had rung for recess. Even Miss Gardner seemed surprised, but quickly gathered herself. "Children, that is the air raid signal. Do just as we have practiced." She then ducked behind her big teacher desk and disappeared! To Odessa's surprise all of the other children were tucking themselves under their desks and were folding themselves into little balls with their hands over their heads.

"Do like I do!!" Nana whispered urgently to her. Odessa quickly complied feeling a little bit scared for some reason. Even Joanne had left her punishment and was quietly mashing herself into a small ball under her desk. You couldn't even see her mouth! No one said a word for about five minutes. It was most uncomfortable.

Finally, the same loud sound came again; Miss Gardner emerged from under her desk, where she had evidently been rolled in a ball just like the children. She stretched and invited the children to come out and stretch as well.

"Very well done, children. We are well prepared and have done our duty. I think we should put away our penmanship and get right to our Spelling Bee."

Odessa was excited. This should be fun! The children lined up on either side of the classroom. She took hold of Nana's hand, but Nana was shaking. She did not look like she was excited at all. In fact, it was obvious that she did not think that a Spelling Bee would be fun. The first words were easy, but still there were children who couldn't spell them and had to sit down. Nana spelled her word very quietly so that Miss Gardner had to stand right in front of her to hear her. Some of the other people giggled. When it got to five children on each side of the room the word that was to be spelled was very easy and it was Nana's turn. All eyes were on her. She was all red and all shaky. Odessa was holding her hand and wanting her to just spell the word and get it over with, but it looked like Nana couldn't open her mouth. Luckily, just then the bell rang and everyone ran out of the room for recess. With a great sigh of relief Nana tightened her hold on Odessa and they followed the class. Miss Gardner didn't say anything.

"What was wrong, Nana?" Odessa asked quietly as she tugged on Nana to hold her back from the others. "Why do you have so much trouble when you know the answers?"

"Odessa, it's hard to explain. Shyness is something you can't just jump out of. I wish I could. If only school could be a place where you get to sit at your desk and no one asks you to stand in front of the class or the group and say anything, I would be fine. I just really don't like everyone looking at me and expecting something. I hope I grow out of it!" Embarrassed at revealing so much she ran to the playground.

"Oh, I think you will," Odessa giggled to herself as she hurried to catch up.

For the last recess the whole class played kickball. Half the class was on one team and the other half formed the other team. The game was played exactly like baseball except instead of using a bat and ball; you used your foot and a kickball. Again, Odessa noticed that Nana hung back and tried not to be 'at bat'. She also played way out in the field rather than on any of the bases. It was as though she didn't want anyone to notice her at all. So weird! By 15 minutes everyone was again hot, sweaty and tired. When they went back into the classroom it didn't take much convincing from Miss Gardner to have everyone put their heads on the desk to listen to a story called "The Princess and the Swan" until the bell rang for dismissal.

"I sure am ready to be at home!" Nana told Odessa as she followed her onto the bus. Odessa started to sit by a red haired little girl, because she wanted to ask her about her bracelet, but Nana sort of shoved her past that seat.

"What was that about, Nana? You would have been in the seat right across from me." She giggled. "No need to get pushy."

"I can't tell you now. Sit down, quickly. Here come the high schoolers."

"Oh, my, they are so big! I guess I wasn't thinking about them this morning. Why are they on the bus with us?"

"Odessa, in the morning the high school people, grades 7 to 12 get on the bus with us, grades 1 to 6 and they come to our school, drop us off and then they go on the bus to the high school. In the afternoon they do the reverse. I like it, because next year Martha will still be on the bus with me. It will be so strange to only have Sam in school with me. I will have to wait until I'm in fourth grade before I'll have Eliott and Sam with me in school. When I get to seventh grade I'll be with Sam and Martha again. It's fun to be able to look around on the playground and always see someone from my family. By the way there is Richard Tabler's stop. He lives in a flat house. There is no upstairs! Everyone gets off the bus before us. We're the last stop."

Finally, Martha, Sam, Nana and Odessa got off the bus. "Okay, Nana," Odessa said. "You have to tell me. Why didn't you want me to sit with that red headed girl? I just wanted to ask her a question about her overalls. I wasn't going to be rude. I promise."

"No. That wasn't the problem at all. I'm sorry you thought that. It is a bit awkward. You see. Miss Gardner told the whole class that Miss Wilkinson told her to tell us not to sit by that girl, because she had cooties. Cooties are these little bugs that get in your hair and can jump from one person's hair to another person. When Miss Wilkinson was a little girl she had cooties and she had to have her hair cut off all the way to bald. One day I did sit with that girl by accident and I didn't want to make her feel bad by getting back up and moving. I worried for days and days that I had caught the cooties and everyone would start not sitting by me. Today I just didn't want you to catch cooties! You have such beautiful hair, and I like to sit by you!"

Martha, Sam and Odessa started to laugh all at once. Sam said, "Maureen, I'm going to make you a cootie catcher. You obviously need one. That old Miss Wilkinson is just a trouble maker. You should just sit by whoever you want. If someone had cooties, they would send her home. You know that check the nurse does when she comes in the classroom and goes around poking a ruler in your hair and then people have to go home?. They are the ones who have cooties. Haven't you noticed that they aren't in school for a couple of weeks and they come back with shorter hair, but are not bald? Kid, you gotta start paying attention!" With that he took off running towards the house.

"He runs a lot, doesn't he?" Odessa guessed. "By the way, what's a 'cootie catcher?'"

"Some days he does run a lot. A cootie catcher is a piece of paper folded up in an intricate way that makes an opening that looks like a mouth. You open and shut it and chase people around pretending to catch cooties from them. How was your day?" Martha asked.

"One thing was confusing. Nana didn't talk much except with her friends, and she didn't want to say much in class or kick the ball in front of the group on the playground. I was kind of surprised because that's the fun part. She doesn't want to be the star at anything."

"There is a little bit of explanation for that. I think I can tell you as her big sister," Martha offered.

"Oh, here we go." Nana put in.

"No, seriously, I have been here your whole life, you know."

"Alright, Miss Smarty-pants, but I'm already saying you're wrong," Nana let her big sister know.

"Here goes. We lived in Washington D.C. until Maureen was four years old. Then our cousin, Larry got Polio, and at the same time there was a Polio epidemic across the country. There were stories of children having to spend their lives in a thing called the iron lung and in wheel chairs like the last President, Franklin Roosevelt. Our parents got nervous about living around possible contagious situations. They decided to move to the farm where their children would have less contact with other children. For more than two years Maureen didn't have any contact with other children except her two brothers and me. We didn't go to stores or anything. When she went to school her class had 35 children and it was quite a shock for her to see that many people in one place. She had always tended to be shy, and now she became super shy. For example, when there was a school play, she couldn't be on the stage, so they gave her the job of pulling the curtain. In other words they find ways to let her do things in her own way."

"Gotta go to the bathroom. See you at the house." Nana yelled as she suddenly ran off.

"I did notice that the teacher moved towards her during the Spelling Bee when she was talking so quietly." Odessa said ignoring Nana's interruption.

"I'm surprised she was in a Spelling Bee. Usually she would be given some other job during something like that. Maybe Miss Gardner thought that with you there, it would give Maureen confidence. Miss Gardner is a tough cookie. Luckily, it's almost the end of the year. Next year Maureen will have Miss Buckley."

"How do you know, already?"

"There is only one class for each grade. My grade only has 22 people. Maureen's class has the most people ever, and first grade has even more. Maureen will have every teacher Sam and I have had. Every time Sam gets to a new grade the teacher thinks he will be just like me. She sure gets a surprise!"

"I can't wait to play with your dogs," Odessa said, spotting the dogs bounding towards them. "How many are there in all?"

"They are all Springer Spaniels. We have just those four right now and 13 puppies. Molly is mine. She has a skin disease called Mange so she isn't very popular, 'cause she stinks. Bonnie belongs to Maureen. She only has one eye. We think a snake bit the other eye. Duke is the boy dog. Penny is a dog that we are keeping for a family who is living somewhere else for awhile where they can't keep dogs. All three girl dogs have puppies that we sell. It is lots of fun thinking of fancy names for them. Our farm is called Lakeland so the puppy names are things like "Sir Buster Lancelot of Lakeland" or Lady Lavender Belle of Lakeland". Bonnie always has the most puppies."

"It sure is a long walk from the bus stop," Odessa told Nana's mother as they came through the screened porch to the kitchen.

"Oh, not so, very far. It keeps you healthy to walk to the bus. Are you hungry? After you change out of your dress, you can help yourself to some peaches that the children's daddy brought home last night."

"Mmmmm....peaches." Nana called from upstairs. "Hurry up and change, Odessa. I'm so hungry, I may eat forty seven!"

Odessa ran up the stairs to the little pink bedroom where Eliott was lounging on the double bed while Nana was changing out of her dress into red shorts.

"Nana, you're changing your clothes in front of a boy!"

"He's not a boy. He's Eliott, my best friend! But Eliott turn over and look out the window while Odessa changes. Count to twenty three. Odessa, you better change fast. He skips a few numbers sometimes."

Odessa changed almost faster than a quick change artist. Martha was changing, too. As they ran downstairs, Odessa noticed that Nana had not bothered to add a shirt to her outfit.

"Nana, you forgot to put on a shirt with your shorts!"

"It's too hot. Eliott isn't wearing one either. We like to be cool. Let me at those peaches. Daddy brought them in last night. Look at this. A whole bushel of peaches! A dream come true!" She was already biting into the first peach. Peach juice dribbled down her chin and settled into her belly button. "Mmmmm….I love peaches so, so much. I've planted so many peach trees with these pits, but they never come up!" She swiped at her tummy as she already finished the first peach, threw the pit on the ground, and reached onto the porch to take another. Odessa was still staring at the first peach wondering if it had been washed. How should she ask? Finally, she decided she may as well just eat it, since she was hungry, too and Nana sure was making it look good. Yum…It was delicious. Little Eliott was eating peaches, too. He was just as messy as Nana. Martha was in the kitchen telling their mommy about school. Their murmur was a steady hum over the peach eaters out in the yard.

"What is that huge pile of orange dirt beside your house," asked Odessa as she tossed her peach pit and picked out another peach.

"That's the dirt that Mac dug out of the basement," Nana told her. Daddy wanted us to have a basement so he asked Mac, a man who works on the farm, to use a shovel and a wheelbarrow to dig the dirt out from under the house. Daddy put cinder blocks around the edges so the house wouldn't fall in the hole that Mac dug, and a big bumblebee truck poured cement to make a floor. The orange dirt is still in the yard. Mommy complains about it, and she and Daddy argue. She wants him to flatten it out with a tractor, but he never does. She doesn't like how it looks, but we all like to dig forts in the dirt."

"Maureen and Odessa, I need you to go and get the eggs," Mommy called from the kitchen handing out a bin.

"Okay, Mommy. I don't think I could eat another peach, now anyway," answered Nana. Odessa noticed that Nana's skinny stomach was now sticking way out. It was funny looking. Nana and Eliott went over to the hose and splashed each other to get the sticky peach juice off of them. Finally, Odessa joined in, because it was better to be splashed than to be hot. It was so hot in 1955!

The three children ran down the hill past the pig pen to the chicken house. Sam was doing something with a long black strip of something nearby. Odessa had to find out what he was up to. "What are you doing?"

"Well, if you have to know, I'm making a belt out of this snake skin. I thought I was doing a really good thing when I killed it. Wouldn't anyone think it was a good thing to kill a snake? But no, not Daddy! He thinks I made some kind of huge mistake. This isn't just any snake. Daddy says this is a 'good' snake, a snake that we need to kill bad creatures that get after the chickens and bother them. Since I made a mistake in killing it, I have to make a belt out of it to make my mistake into a good thing. Anyway, in this boiling hot sun, I have to scrape and scrape this stupid thing and turn it into a belt. Now, does that make any little bit of sense to you?" he asked angrily.

Odessa didn't know what the right answer was to his question. Luckily, she didn't have to answer, because Eliott was fascinated with the process of working with the snake skin and had lots of questions for the annoyed Sam. Odessa and Nana crept over to the chicken house.

"When we go into the chicken house, you take the eggs out of the empty nests. When there is a chicken sitting on her nest, you slip your hand under the chicken and take the egg out from under her. Try to slip under her from the back, because if you go from the front, she may peck you."

"Um, Nana, how about if you do the nests with the chickens on them. I don't think I'm ready for that."

"Okay, hold your shirt up in front and I'll put them in it"

"Wait, Nana, what is that stuff on the eggs?"

"Chicken doo doo. Don't worry. It washes off. All the eggs have to be washed. Anyway, no one eats the shells, Odessa."

"Then, let's not put them in my shirt. Let's put them in that pan your Mom gave you. Yeouck! Why do they do that?"

"Odessa, think about it. They are sitting right on the eggs. Okay, let's not talk about it."

They finished collecting the eggs and gave them to Sam to take to the house since he was on his way up.

"Do you want to see our lambs, Sydney and Arthur?"

"Sure"

Eliott, Nana, and Odessa went over to the lamb pen where two lambs were ambling around. They went in and sat down with the lambs on their laps. Eliott and Nana told about the neighbors who had given them the lambs several months before.

"I wish you had been here when we were feeding them with bottles. It was so much fun. They are so cuddly, but they are not like dogs. They don't know their names or their masters. They just wander around, but are soft and cozy to hug when they are little."

"Let's go see my kitty, Rachel. Eliott and I usually find her up in the hay loft. Right now there isn't much hay up there, because it has mostly been all thrown down for the cattle. You walk down this hallway that divides the barn into two halves. The horses use one half when they come in to eat, and the two cows come in the other side to be milked. Right now we have one horse, Lady and a pony named Prince. Prince nips, so stay away from him. Lady is so, so sweet. We love to curry her and hug her. She smells really cozy. Anyway, the ladder to the hayloft is at the end of this hallway."

Odessa looked around. She really wanted to get a chance to look Lady, the horse over and maybe even get a whiff of that cozy smell. "Where are Prince and Lady?"

c)Kreefax/Dreamstime.com Dairy Cows in a herd photo

"They're out in the pasture. The cows are out there, too with the rest of the cattle. They all like to eat the grass when it is a nice day like this. The other barn is for hanging tobacco. The animals don't go in there. Be careful when you climb the ladder. You have to kind of lift yourself off the last rung into the hayloft."

"See that big hole over there. That's where the hay bales are pushed out to the cattle. Here, kitty, kitty. Here, kitty, kitty. Sometimes Rachel hides if she just had kittens. We like to find them and play with them, but the next time we come down, she's hidden them all over again. There she is!"

Odessa saw a beautiful tabby cat come out from behind a bale in the corner. Forgetting that she was allergic to cats, Odessa sat right down on the floor and Rachel walked over and leaned on her chest purring loudly.

"Isn't she the sweetest kitty you've ever seen?" Rachel rolled over and let all three children pet her as she purred and purred.

"She sure does love attention!" Odessa had to say.

"Not as much as we love giving it to her!" Nana exclaimed. The children took turns looking all around the hayloft to see if there were any kittens, but if there were any, Rachel had hidden them well.

Odessa was starting to sneeze which reminded Nana that Odessa was allergic to cats so she suggested; "it's getting hot up here. Let's play with the puppies and then cool off in the creek before dinner." They climbed down the ladder and headed to the puppy pen where Sam and Martha were already playing. They had put on coats and had also brought one for Eliott, because they were thinking of going black berry picking and didn't want to get chigger bites.

The puppies crawled all over everyone and licked everybody's faces, hands and ears. People and puppies were rolling left and right. With thirteen puppies there were more than enough to go around for the five children. Finally, when the puppies started to go off and snooze, Eliott, Nana, and Odessa headed for the creek while Sam and Martha went in search of blackberries for dinner.

Odessa had been surprised that everyone didn't mind walking around barefooted. Now she saw the advantages as Eliott and Nana were first to wade into the creek and let out a loud "Aaaah!" She quickly took off her shoes and gingerly tiptoed after them. The water was very cold and felt so good. To her surprise it wasn't two seconds before both Nana and Eliott were sitting smack dab in the middle of the creek. Well... Why not? It was just as cool as it looked. "Aaaah!!!"

Next, they spent some time floating various objects down the creek. It turned out that leaves from certain trees floated faster than from other trees and that green leaves didn't float as well as brown leaves. They experimented with sticks of different sizes, too.

At one point Eliott found a dead frog so, of course, they had to have a funeral for him. His name was Mister Sir Frogster. Eliott dug a hole and sang a nice song. Nana made up a poem for him and Odessa said a lovely prayer. Eliott then made a tombstone of a large rock. They decorated the grave with wildflowers. It was all very moving.

After that, they dug a trench in the creek to see if they could make the creek into a swimming pool for Bonnie, Nana's dog, who had come to join them after her puppies were all napping. She helped by digging, too, but she dug so energetically that she made herself all muddy. Then they decided to give her a bath which made them even wetter than she was.

About this time Odessa whispered to Nana, "I have to go to the bathroom."

"No problem. There's a three holer down by the red barn. I have to go, too. Come on, Eliott. We're going to the bathroom."

"Why is Eliott coming?"

"Because he's my best friend!"

When they got to the little brown building, Odessa was dismayed at what it looked like on the outside, but she was even more astounded when she saw the inside. Before they went in though, Nana told Eliott to march up and down outside the door and be the guard for their bathroom castle. He used a stick as his weapon, raised it to his shoulder and began to march. Inside there were three holes the size of bottoms on a bench. Odessa did not look inside the holes. Nana had already pulled down her little red shorts and was sitting on one of the holes. "It is very companionable," Nana said. "Martha and I often have very good conversations in here. Of course, that's when we don't have the curious bathroom castle guard outside. Mommy says when she was little they had to use catalogues as toilet paper in the outhouse. Isn't that strange?"

Odessa didn't want to comment just at that moment what she thought was strange so she kept her thoughts to herself and did what had to be done.

Just as they came out of the outhouse they heard a loud voice calling "Dinnnnneeeeerrrr!"

Their castle guard deserted his post and ran up to the house. They ran quickly after him.

Martha was washing lettuce at the hose. "Mommy wants you to go and pull 15 onions and wash them for dinner. Then you are to set the table. By then everything will be ready. I could eat a horse."

The girls ran out into the garden and quickly pulled 15 spring onions, washed them at the hose, and delivered them to Mommy in the kitchen. Odessa noticed that the kitchen was very unusual. It was a long kitchen with a sink at one end and wooden crates set on their sides up and down the length of the room. Red curtains were tacked on the front of the crates to hide the dishes and pans.

Odessa and Nana gathered seven plates, glasses, spoons, forks, knives, cloth napkins and napkin rings and took them to the dining room where they set the table in the same arrangement as breakfast had been served. Nana explained that everyone always sat in exactly the same seat. She told Odessa that the kitchen cabinets were not finished yet and were actually sitting at the end of the living room. Odessa peeked in the living room and sure enough a huge area of the living room was full of objects covered in sheets. It looked like they had been there a long time, because things were on top of them.

Before everyone came to dinner Nana, Sam, and Eliott went upstairs and put on shirts. Nana explained that her mother wouldn't let anyone eat who didn't have a shirt on. Everyone sat down at the same time, and a whole mountain of food appeared. There was a big platter of meat, and bowls of mashed potatoes, string beans, stewed tomatoes, apple sauce and a large wooden boat-like container of salad. As the food was passed around, some of each thing was placed on Odessa's plate. No one asked if she wanted this or that, it just got put on her plate. A huge glass of milk was again in front of her. She was, of course, willing to try everything, but she was worried she wouldn't like something. Then what would she do?

Conversation began about the new baby that was to arrive in late July or August. Nana was convinced it would be a girl. Her argument made lots of sense to everyone else. Their family had started with a girl, boy, girl, boy sequence. Their cousins' families had also alternated either girl, boy as in Aunt Maureen's family, boy, girl, boy in Aunt Sally's family and boy, girl in Aunt Randy's family.

"Yes, there is no question that the new baby will be a girl. Mommy, you promise you will name her Mary. I really want a little sister to spoil, Nana told her mother. Eliott is a great best friend, but I want a little sister, now."

"Sweetheart, no one can tell in advance whether a baby will be a boy or a girl. We just have to wait and see. Mary is a beautiful name, though. Remember, that you can pick a middle name for yourself any time you want to. Maybe, Mary is the one you should choose," her mother commented.

"No, I don't want to have a middle name yet. If I get one, then it will be over and I won't have the fun ever again of getting to choose it. I'll be just like everyone else. I'm still thinking it over. Besides I don't want to steal my little sister's name. Right, Odessa?"

"Wellllll," said Odessa. She knew she wasn't allowed to give anything away, but it sure was hard not to say anything about the future. (She managed just barely to keep to herself that the next baby would be named Harry.) "Mary sounds like a name that would be just about right for the next person in your family. That's for sure."

"Yum. This apple sauce is delicious." She tried to distract them. "Where did you buy it?"

"Buy it!" They all laughed, but Sam was the one who told her. "We didn't buy anything on the table. We grew everything ourselves. Some of the vegetables Mommy canned and kept in jars over the winter. The other things have just started coming up in the garden. In the summer we pick everything fresh and eat it the same day. My favorite thing to get is the potatoes. The tractor plows up the field where they grow underground and then we go and pick them up. It's kind of like they were playing hide and seek. Then the apples, onions and potatoes stay in the basement in bins during the winter."

Odessa looked around soon after and discovered that there wasn't a morsel left on anyone's plate, but hers. What was she to do? Evidently, it wasn't a problem. They cleared the table and her plate was scraped into a big bucket of garbage which stood by the door. "Where is your dishwasher?" She asked, looking around.

"There she is," Nana answered pointing to her mommy and throwing Odessa a dishtowel. "And she has five dish dryers. Sam, don't flip your towel at Odessa. It hurts and she isn't used to you!"

"I wouldn't do that to Odessa, Maureen. Just to you!" He cried as he chased a screeching Nana around the kitchen. Eliott chased them both.

"Samuel Thomas Robertson! There will be none of that!" His mother's voice had him skidding to a halt.

"We have a game," Martha told Odessa amid the commotion. "If Mommy gets ten dishes or utensils in the drying rack before we can dry them she wins, and if we get the rack empty we win."

As the family washed and dried the dishes their mother quizzed them on the capitals of the states. Then they sang songs. There were ones that Odessa knew like "Working on the Railroad" and others she didn't know. She especially liked the ones that they sang in rounds like "Frere Jacques" and "Row, Row your Boat". Nana's Mommy was a very good singer.

"Let's sing "My Bonnie Lies over the Ocean". That's my favorite 'cause Bonnie's my dog," Nana insisted.

They all sang:

My Bonnie lies over the ocean,
My Bonnie lies over the sea,
My Bonnie lies over the ocean
Oh bring back my Bonnie to me.

Then they sang another favorite one their granddaddy had taught them.

I saw the boat go 'round the bend
Loaded down with railroad men
Good-bye my lover good-bye
Bye baby bye ee o
Bye baby bye ee o
Good bye my lover good bye.

At a certain point they realized that they were all standing around the kitchen holding what they called "tea towels" and the dishes had been done for awhile.

"Don't you hate doing the dishes?" Sam said to Eliott and the two boys stomped out.

With the dishwashing over, Nana's mommy said, "Martha, you, Maureen and Odessa can slop the pigs, tonight. Take this bucket. Right after that we'll listen to a radio program and then it will be bedtime for these little girls."

Martha picked up the heavy bucket of garbage that had been gathered all day long. Odessa saw potato and carrot peels and a lot of other stuff she did not want to identify. Nana carried a smaller bucket and Odessa carried a bag which smelled awful. They hiked down the hill to the pigpen.

"They sure are happy to see us!" Odessa called out over the loud snorting and snuffling of the pigs. What happened to 'oink'? Did they forget what they are supposed to say?"

As Martha and the girls dumped the slop into the trough the pigs climbed all over each other trying to get to the food. "Wow, they're such, well, pigs!" Odessa laughed. "I've never seen anything like it. So that's where the expression about eating like a pig comes from. They are hilarious!" She reached down and touched the back of one of the pigs. His hair was bristly, sparse and coated with mud. He didn't even notice that she had touched him. Pigs were the funniest animal she had seen today and that even included that silly Joanne from Nana's school!

The girls trudged back up the hill to the house and went into the large living room. The old house had been used for a barn for many years before Nana's family had decided to use it as a home. They had knocked down a wall between two rooms to make the living room very large. At one end of the room were the sheet covered kitchen cabinets. A big fireplace dominated the other end of the room with two small bookcases on either side. There were two couches, a few easy chairs and some rugs over a hardwood floor. Because there were no steps up to the front door which was in the middle of the room, it was not used. Everyone came into the house through the kitchen. As Odessa, Martha and Nana entered the living room, they saw that Nana's Mommy was ironing and the boys were wrestling on the floor.

"You are just in time. 'The Lone Ranger' is about to start on the radio." A box the size of a toaster was sitting on a short bookcase that Odessa recognized from her aunt's house in the future. The box had two round knobs on it. Martha fiddled with the two knobs and the show came on. The girls lay on the floor, too and put their feet on the furniture. It was surprisingly comfortable. The Lone Ranger had a pal named Tonto and a horse named Silver. They saved the day without much trouble. All the children yelled, "Hiyo Silver!" quite a few times and sang along with the only advertisement which was about something people put on their hair to make it shiny and smooth."Brill Cream, a little dab'll do yah". It was catchy.

Lying on the floor had made Odessa snoozy. She was not at all reluctant to go up to bed. Eliott had already changed and was on Nana's bed with his back turned counting to twenty-nine while she and Nana changed into their pajamas. He didn't want to miss a thing. Unfortunately, the little guy fell asleep counting and was carried off to his own bed.

Finally, Odessa was again snuggled in bed with Carrot safe in her arms. She felt Nana's cozy warmth behind her. Nana had her skinny arm around Odessa's tummy and was leaning her head on Odessa's hair. Martha, Nana's Mommy and Nana sang Odessa's special song:

Dessie are you okay.
Are you okay, Dessie?

What a nice day it had been. She thought she would just rest her eyes for a minute.

Dessie are you okay.
Are you okay, Dessieeeee?

She opened her eyes back up after only what seemed seconds later. Where was the small pink room? This wasn't little Nana's skinny arm! This was Mom's arm! There was Dad! And Stella! And Rigsby!!! They were the ones singing to her! She jumped straight up in her bed.

"Mom, Dad, Stella! You'll never guess what happened?!!! Nana got her wish! I went back and visited her in her second grade! Wait till I tell you all about it!"

Rigsby and Stella started leaping all around the room just as excited as she was. "I have news, too, Odessa!" Stella shouted gleefully. "I decided to be a wishing Nana, too! I wished for my granddaughter to visit too! The only rule is that she can't tell us anything about the future. She'll be here tomorrow. Her name is Megan Rose! She's coming from the year 2070! I can't wait! I can't wait!"

Printed in the United States
By Bookmasters